Fishing Small Rivers and Streams

PAUL DUFFIELD

Copyright © 2014 Paul Duffield

All rights reserved.

ISBN-10: 1500617490
ISBN-13: 978-1500617493

CONTENTS

INTRODUCTION	1
FISHING SMALL RIVERS AND STREAMS	3
TACKLE	9
TROTTING FOR DACE AND ROACH	17
TACTICS FOR LARGE ROACH	21
TACTICS FOR CHUB	23
TACTICS FOR BARBEL	28
TACTICS FOR PERCH	33
TACTICS FOR PIKE	38
FUN WITH GUDGEON AND MINNOWS	44
JUNGLE SWIMS	46
FISHING IN FLOOD CONDITIONS	49
A LESS SELECTIVE APPROACH	53
SMALL RIVER TECHNIQUES AND RIGS	55
USEFUL KNOTS	75
BAITS FOR SMALL RIVER FISHING	81
LICENCES AND PERMISSION TO FISH	84

INTRODUCTION

With so many well stocked commercial carp fisheries available these days, rivers, especially small streams and the tributaries of larger rivers, see far fewer anglers if any at all, than was the case 20 or more years ago.

It's true that small rivers and streams don't offer easy fishing with the prospect of several plump 5lb to 10lb carp hooked and banked at the end of the day, but with light tackle, a chub or perch of a few pounds or a roach pushing the pound mark can put up just as exciting a fight.

Watercraft, by which I mean being able to read a swim to work out what fish it is likely to contain, where they are likely to be and the best approach to catch them, plays a large part too. The fish in such places are wild and have never been hand fed and fattened up in fish farms.

Fishing small rivers and streams requires different tackle and a different approach to commercial stillwater fisheries and usually a longer walk too, but the sense of achievement that capturing a wily 3lb chub or glistening 1lb roach from its own natural environment can bring, is miles away from pulling carp after carp out of an artificial pond.

You don't need a lot of expensive tackle to start small river fishing, if you're already a coarse angler you probably have most of what you need already, so why not give it a try? It will add variety and another dimension to your sport and might just become your favourite style of fishing.

FISHING SMALL RIVERS AND STREAMS

You can catch fish in small rivers and streams all through the season in all but the worst floods, but different tactics are required to suit the time of year and condition of the river.

Even the smallest streams can contain surprisingly large fish in the deeper pools, while rivers that are almost narrow enough to jump across with a depth of a just a few feet can hold large shoals of fish.

For the smallest streams where rapid shallow areas give way to the occasional deeper pool usually on tree lined bends, a light legering approach is called for, while float fishing tactics can be successful on stretches of small rivers where there is a swim of a few yards or more of uniform depth.

On small rivers, especially those that contain large shoals of roach and dace, a careful approach and consistent feeding can keep fish coming for several hours.

If the larger fish are your quarry, a selective approach with large baits can bring results, while a less selective approach trotting a small bait under a stick float can provide hectic sport.

On the smallest streams playing and landing a large fish in a small swim alerts other fish in the swim to danger and there is little chance of another for a while, so you will need to adopt a roving approach and fish several different swims.

On a small river you are never far away from the fish, so it can be difficult to catch fish in a clear low river, but as soon as there is a little colour in the water, such as when the river is fining down after a flood, some excellent sport can be had.

On many of the small rivers I have fished, swims that appear devoid of fish on days when the river is so low and clear that you can make out individual stones on the bottom, have produced many excellent days of sport when the river is coloured and carrying a few extra inches of water.

Small river fishing will be a little different to the fishing you are used to if you have only fished stillwaters, so I'll start with some general advice.

CASTING A LEGER

A leger rig can be cast overhand, but often a simple pendulum swing will be best as it can be done in front of the body in the tightest of swims.

Let out enough line so that you can comfortably swing the rig by lifting and lowering the rod, point the rod in the direction you wish to cast and when you have built up momentum, release the line before you complete an outward swing.

Timing of this cast is critical, but with practice you will be able to drop the rig accurately and gently into the water.

CASTING A FLOAT

Floats for river fishing are usually attached top and bottom and are best cast underhand rather than the overhead cast used with bottom only floats on stillwaters. This cast can be performed in tight swims with more control and less risk of tangles.

To begin the cast, assuming you are right handed, hold the rod in your right hand, open the bail arm of the reel, and let out enough line from the rod tip so that with your left hand you can comfortably hold the line just above the hook.

Hold the rod across your body while keeping the line under tension with your left hand, and then flick the rod towards the water so that it is pointing directly away from you, at the same time releasing the line held in your left hand. You should find that the tackle is propelled towards the place you want to fish and if you get enough power into the cast and get your timing right, line should flow off the spool.

Timing of this cast can be difficult to master, but with practice you will find that it becomes second nature. As your skills progress you will find that you can achieve this cast holding the rod at different angles to avoid bank side vegetation and other obstacles.

TROTTING THE SWIM

If you have only ever float fished on a stillwater fishery, you will find float fishing on rivers to be quite different and in all likelihood, quite difficult at first.

When stillwater float fishing, you may have to contend with drift and wind, but on a river you need to be able to control the float during its passage down the swim so that the bait behaves naturally.

The float will be carried by the current and follow the route of the body of water it is floating in, but the line trailing behind the float must be controlled so that it does not drag the float off course and make the bait behave differently to other food moving down the river.

If the line catches a surface current and is dragged to the side or ahead of the float, the float will be pulled out of position, so you need to keep a fairly tight line to the float at all times while still allowing the float to travel at the speed of the current by paying out line.

You do this by leaving the bail arm of the reel open and releasing line under slight tension, controlled by pressure applied with your finger at the edge of the spool.

To keep a tight line to the float you may need to 'mend the line' by trapping the line with your finger and lifting the rod until the line between the rod tip and float is straight. On rivers where the flow is slow and there are many surface currents you may need to do this several times on each passage of the float down the swim.

This technique is referred to as 'trotting', and when the float needs to travel a long way down the swim to reach the fish, it is known as 'long trotting'.

When you get a bite, you trap the line against the spool with your finger and strike with a sweeping movement away from the float. The further away the float is, the more powerful the strike, but often it is only necessary to stop the float as the current will set the hook.

As soon as a fish is hooked you have to decide whether you need to allow it to take line, before you close the bail arm of the reel in preparation for winding in or playing the fish.

If it is a small fish you can immediately close the bail arm and commence winding. If you feel resistance from a large fish, allow it to take line with the bail arm open and close it when you feel the fish stop its initial run.

When fishing with running line tackle on rivers, make sure that the anti-reverse on the reel is set to the off position if you intend to give line by winding backwards rather than using the slipping clutch.

FINDING THE DEPTH OF YOUR SWIM

When float fishing you need to know the depth of the swim so you can trot through with your bait just off or just tripping along the bottom, which is where the fish will most often be.

If you are fishing a slow moving river, the depth of the swim can be found using a plummet, but on faster moving water a plummet cannot be used as the float will be pulled under by the flow.

Set the float at your best guess of the depth and run the float through the swim several times, adjusting the depth each time until the hook catches on the river bed and the float is pulled under.

Finally slide the float back towards the float a little and run the float though the swim again to make sure that it will reach the end of the swim without the hook catching on the bottom.

Some swims can vary in depth throughout their length. Here you have two choices:

- Set the float to a depth that will allow the hook to clear the bottom throughout the length of the swim.

- Set the float to a depth where it will only catch the bottom occasionally, and as the float reaches those areas hold it back slightly to cause the hook to rise above the bottom until the float has passed into deeper water.

FEEDING THE SWIM

Feeding a swim on a river is quite different to feeding a swim on a stillwater.

Depending on the depth of the swim and the strength of the current, your bait could reach the river bed anywhere from just past the point at which you introduce it, to a significant distance down the river.

Over time you will develop a feel for where in the swim, or even above it, you will need to introduce free offerings, but as a general guide, the faster the flow and the deeper the swim, the further upstream you will need to introduce bait.

As a general rule when float fishing you should feed every cast just before you cast so that your hook bait is travelling among the free offerings.

You should aim for your bait to reach the bottom of the river about two thirds of the way down the swim. The bait will continue to move with the current after it reaches the bottom, but by this time your hook bait should also be traveling near the bottom.

By feeding 'little and often' you will attract fish into the swim and keep them there. Over feeding risks fish chasing off downstream after excess bait.

It may take some time for you to start getting bites if there are few fish in the swim to begin with, but eventually fish should be drawn upstream by your loose feed and once they are in the swim, feeding small amounts of bait regularly should keep them there.

PLAYING LARGE FISH IN CONFINED SWIMS

In confined swims, fish are never far away from a snag that could cause you to lose the fish, so at times you will have to clamp down tight to prevent the fish taking line.

In very tight swims where you have to turn a fish quickly if it runs for a snag, it is best to fully tighten the clutch and give line when necessary by back winding the reel.

Applying side strain by holding the rod almost parallel to the water will often help to turn a fish more effectively than by holding the rod high.

Be aware of your surroundings, in particular any nearby trees and bushes that the rod tip or line could become tangled in when striking or playing a fish.

TACKLE

When fishing small rivers you will often be walking quite long distances and on some rivers you will be changing swims regularly so it pays to carry as little tackle as possible.

I prefer to only carry a single rod and use it for both float fishing and legering. Although this means I don't have the benefit of a sensitive quiver tip, I'm happy to compromise for the extra mobility.

RODS

Rods for small river fishing need to be shorter than for other waters as you will often be fishing in confined swims. A rod of 10ft to 11ft is short enough to use where space is restricted and is long enough to comfortably control a float in moving water.

At one time it was difficult to find a rod of that length with a sensitive enough tip for float fishing, but the pellet waggler rods introduced in recent years for use on carp fisheries are ideal. They combine power in the butt section capable of subduing quite large fish, with a sensitive tip that protects light hook lengths and is good for bite detection when legering too.

Such a rod will be fine for most small river fishing, but if the river you intend to fish has large chub or barbel present, an Avon rod with a test curve around 1.25 lb to 1.75lb would be a better choice.

REELS AND LINE

Any small fixed spool reel will be suitable, preferably with one or two spare spools so you have a choice of line strengths. For float fishing and most legering, main line of 3lb to 3.5lb (1.3kg to 1.5kg) will be suitable. For legering in snaggy swims for chub and barbel, line of about 6lb (2.7kg) will be needed and if you intend to fish for pike, you will need main line of 10lb to 12lb (4.5kg to 5.5kg).

Unless you only intend to use hooks already tied to line, a selection of line for hook lengths will also be needed in breaking stains .5lb to 1lb (.25kg to .5kg) less than your main lines.

NETS, LUGGAGE AND SEATING

Complete your tackle with a rod rest or two, a landing net - the flip up type used by trout anglers are ideal for a roving approach, a selection of terminal tackle (see below) in a small tackle box, a compact unhooking mat and a small shoulder bag or rucksack to carry it in along with some food and drink.

I prefer not to take a rod holdall or quiver to cut down on weight, but on days when rain is likely, I take a 36inch umbrella and use a small quiver to carry it along with the rod rests and landing net.

What you sit on is up to you. I prefer to carry a lightweight roving chair, but a simple stool will be fine if you find it comfortable enough, or you could just sit on an unhooking mat.

TERMINAL TACKLE AND OTHER ITEMS

The following items are needed to construct the rigs and use the methods described in later chapters of this book.

STICK FLOATS

Stick floats are the most widely used floats for fishing rivers. These are floats constructed in two parts, the top part being of balsa or polystyrene and the bottom of either cane, plastic or wire.

Generally speaking, the further you need to cast, the larger the float you will use, but a small range of stick floats in four or five sizes will be enough to get you started. Avoid the smallest and largest of this type of float, and obtain a few ranging in size from 4 to 6 inches

(10cm to 15cm) in length.

BALSA FLOATS

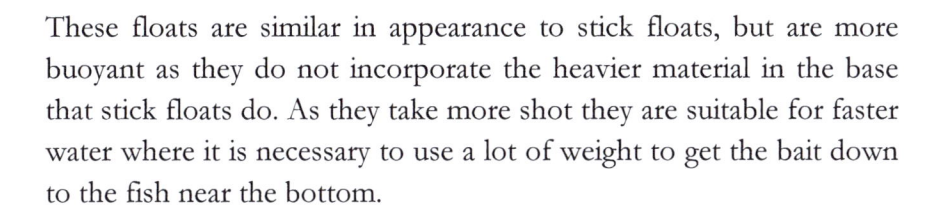

These floats are similar in appearance to stick floats, but are more buoyant as they do not incorporate the heavier material in the base that stick floats do. As they take more shot they are suitable for faster water where it is necessary to use a lot of weight to get the bait down to the fish near the bottom.

A range of balsa floats in lengths from 4 to 6 inches (10cm to 15cm) will cover most of your angling needs.

AVON FLOATS

These are floats that incorporate a large body of balsa, polystyrene or cork to increase the amount of shot that can be placed on the line. These are mostly used in deeper swims where their extra shot capacity is needed to get the bait down to the fish as quickly as possible.

You will not use these as often as stick floats and balsas, but it is useful to have two or three just in case. A range with shot capacities ranging from 4BB to 6BB will cover most eventualities.

CHUBBER FLOATS

The chubber float is basically a version of the balsa float that is scaled up in width but not length. They carry a much larger amount of shot than a balsa float and are designed primarily to be used with large baits such as lobworms or bread.

SHOT

You will need a range of shot in various sizes to give maximum versatility in shotting floats.

There is a wide range of non-toxic shot available, but make sure that you get a good quality brand of soft shot which can usually be identified by a light grey colour. This is less likely to damage line and is easier to remove for re-use.

The sizes most commonly used are SSG, AAA, BBB, Number 1, Number 4, Number 6 and Number 8. You should have no trouble obtaining a single dispenser containing most or all of these sizes.

It is still legal to use lead in size 8 and smaller, but for the larger sizes you must use a non-toxic alternative to lead.

HOOKS

Hook sizes and patterns need to be chosen to match the species of fish and size of bait you intend to use. As a general guide, a selection in sizes 20, 18, 16, 14, 12, 10, 8 and 6 will cover most of your small river fishing.

FLOAT CAPS

You will need some plastic or silicon tubing in various thicknesses to attach floats to the line. These are sometimes described as 'float caps' or 'float rubbers'.

You can either buy a packet of pre-cut tubing in mixed sizes, or obtain lengths of plastic or silicon tubing to cut to size when needed.

PLUMMETS

These are small weights incorporating either a strip of cork or a hinge to hold the hook while lowering the tackle into the swim so you can set the float at the correct depth.

LEGER WEIGHTS

Leger weights are attached to the line to allow a bait to be presented on or near the bed of a river or lake. You will need a range of sizes to cover differences in river flow and the distance you need to cast.

There are many types of leger weight. the most versatile are pear shaped weight incorporating a swivel, known as Arlesey Bombs and a flattened version designed to hold the bottom in strong flows.

A selection of these in weights from .25 to 1 oz (7 to 28 grams) will meet most of your small river fishing needs.

SWIMFEEDERS

Swimfeeders are devices that take the place of leger weights and incorporate a means of getting free offerings of your hook bait or groundbait to the place where you are fishing.

Broadly speaking there are two types, those than are closed at both ends and are mostly used for delivering maggots to the swim and those that are open at both ends and are used to deliver a mix of groundbait and maggots, pellets or other baits.

LEGER STOPS

Leger stops are used to prevent leger weights from sliding down the line towards the hook.

FLOAT STOPS

Float stops can be used in place of stop knots for sliding float rigs and are also useful for making up semi-fixed leger rigs.

BAIT BANDS

These are silicon bands available in a range of sizes that can be used to attach hard baits such pellets, or large baits such as bread flake to the hook.

SWIVELS

Swivels help to avoid line twist and are used with some specialist carp fishing float rigs.

RUBBER BEADS

Rubber beads are used as a shock absorber with some specialist carp fishing float rigs.

BAITING NEEDLE

If you intend to use hair rigs, a baiting needle with a small hook near the point will be needed to thread baits such as boilies or pellets on to the hair.

BAIT STOPS

Bait stops are used to trap baits against the loop of a hair rig.

DISGORGERS

You should always carry a few disgorgers for use when a fish has swallowed the hook.

FORCEPS

Forceps are a useful unhooking tool for removing large hooks.

PIKE FISHING TACKLE AND ACCESSORIES

If you intend to fish for pike you will also need the following items.

PENCIL FLOATS AND INLINE FLOATS

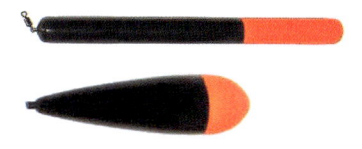

Pencil floats (top) and inline floats (bottom) are used for float fishing and legering for pike.

WIRE TRACES

Wire traces are essential for pike fishing. These either incorporate one or two treble hooks for live and dead bait fishing, or a swivel for attaching spinners and lures.

POLYBALLS/BAIT POPPERS

Polyballs are buoyant polystyrene balls used to construct popped up and paternoster pike rigs.

LONG FORCEPS

A long pair of forceps (10in. to 12in. / 25cm to 30cm) is useful for removing hooks from pike when the hook is deep inside the mouth or throat.

PLIERS

A small pair of pliers can sometimes be better for unhooking pike than forceps.

UNHOOKING GLOVE

Pike have sharp teeth so an unhooking glove can be useful for protecting your hands when removing hooks.

LARGE LANDING NET

For most small river fishing a large landing net is not required, but if you are intending to target large pike, make you have a net that is large enough.

TROTTING FOR DACE AND ROACH

If you can find a swim on the river with a uniform depth of two feet (60cm) or more for several yards, there is a good possibility that shoals of dace or roach are present.

Often these shoals mainly consist of fish of no more than a few ounces, but larger fish can be present among them and not knowing what will take your bait from one cast to the next makes this an exciting form of fishing.

Trotting or 'swimming the stream' as this method used to be known, is an active form of fishing that takes practice to learn, but will often result in more fish on the bank than leger or swimfeeder tactics.

Before fishing with a bait on the hook, run the float through the swim a few times to determine the depth and set the float to run through the swim with the bait just off the bottom.

Start by running the float through the swim at the speed of the current, mending line as necessary to keep the float on track. The bail arm of the reel should be left open and line released using gentle finger pressure on the edge of the spool.

It can pay to hold the float back momentarily from time to time so the bait lifts off the bottom and to hold back for a second or two at the end of the swim before winding in.

Running the float through under gentle pressure so that it travels a little slower than the current can work on days when the fish are less inclined to bite. With practice this can be done with a fixed spool reel, but many anglers prefer a centrepin reel for this style of fishing.

You should feed a few samples of your hook bait just before each cast so your baited hook travels among the free samples. On a medium paced river, bait can be thrown in just above the point where you cast the float, while on faster swims bait should be introduced further upstream.

Maggots are a good bait for this method and can produce bites almost immediately. Other small bait such as casters or pellets can work too, but it may take longer for the fish to switch on to the bait.

Tackle should be light, a main line of about 3lb (1.36kg) with a lighter hook length of 2.5lb (1.1kg) or less and a size 18 hook should be suitable for most swims, but you may need to use a lighter hook length and smaller hook in very clear water.

Bites will often be registered by the float diving below the surface, but these are by no means un-missable and require a quick strike, especially with dace. Sometimes the float will just appear to stop moving with the current or move a little to the side.

Any unusual behaviour of the float is a signal to strike, but there is no need to strike too hard, just a firm flick is all that is needed. If you miss a bite, the float can be allowed to continue to the end of the swim before retrieving to re-cast.

Depending on the strength of the flow, either a stick float or balsa rig will be suitable, the stick float rig with spaced out shot working best for medium flows, the balsa rig with bulked shot being best when the current is stronger.

In the diagram below, the first two are stick float rigs for slow to medium flows and the third is a balsa rig for faster flows. These are explained in more detail in the rigs chapter later in this book.

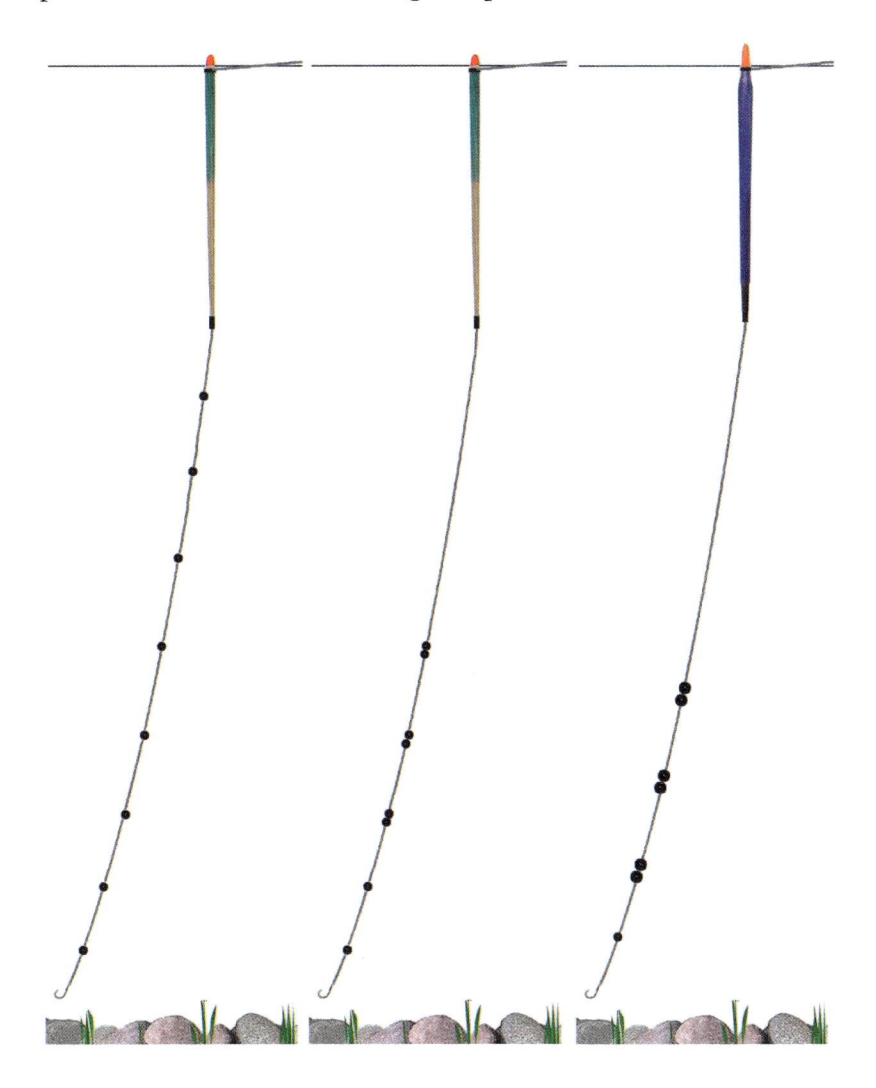

When you hook a small fish, the bail arm can be closed and the fish reeled gently in, but if you hook one of the larger specimens, be prepared to give line using finger pressure on the spool and close the bail arm after the initial run.

Larger fish are often found in slacker water just off the main current.

Holding back hard when the float is about half way down the swim so that it is pulled into the near bank can often result in quite savage bites from the larger fish in the shoal.

TACTICS FOR LARGE ROACH

On small rivers where roach are present in reasonable numbers, a large roach, by which I mean any roach of 1lb or more in weight, is a realistic target.

Swims with cover such as overhanging trees where the river deepens and is a little slower than the average flow are where large roach will often be found. Areas of slacker water just off the main current along beds of reeds are also good large roach holding areas.

Larger than average roach can often be caught when trotting for roach and dace as explained in the previous chapter, but selectively targeting large roach requires a different tactic.

While they can be caught at any time of the day, early morning and from late afternoon are the most productive times for large roach during the warmer months. In autumn and winter the best time to try is from late afternoon to dusk, especially at the end of a mild day.

As is often the case with small river fishing, larger fish, including roach, feed more confidently when there is a little colour in the water.

In terms of bait, bread flake takes some beating for large roach. Although float fishing can be successful, legering a large piece of flake on a size 8 to 12 hook tied direct to a main line of 3lb to 3.5lb (1.3kg to 1.5kg) with a simple link leger rig is usually a more productive method.

If the river you are fishing contains large chub you may need to step up to a stronger main line. Chub are comfortable in the sort of swims that are favoured by large roach and they will also take bread flake just as readily.

Mashed bread should be introduced to the swim before fishing, but be careful not to introduce too much as bread is a filling bait and there are not likely to be large numbers of fish in the swim. Two or three walnut sized balls is fine to start with, topped up from time to time.

If you are able to get to the water on days you are not fishing, pre-baiting a swim regularly will get the fish used to finding bread in the swim and feeding on it confidently.

While a sensitive quivertip is an advantage, bites will often be a strong and confident pull, but you need to be ready to strike so hold the rod when waiting for a bite.

I find the easiest and most comfortable way to do this is to place the rod on a rest with the butt section supported on my leg and my hand resting on the rod at the reel.

If you prefer touch legering to watching the rod tip, loop the line over your index finger just in front of the reel and be ready to strike when you feel a steady pull or sharp tug on the line.

TACTICS FOR CHUB

If you want to hook a fish that will put a bend in your rod and put up a spirited fight, the chub is your best bet on most small rivers.

Chub can grow surprisingly large in even the smallest streams and my first encounter with a fish over 2lbs was on a river that for most of its length was less than 6 inches deep with the odd deeper pool where the depth increased to a couple of feet.

I prefer to fish for chub in autumn and winter when the river is coloured and carrying a little extra water, but you can catch chub from small rivers at any time of the year with a quiet and careful approach.

Typical chub swims combine a steady flow with a reasonable depth of water and overhead cover. Extra depth and a slower steady flow often go hand in hand, but as a general rule it is best to avoid swims where the surface water is uneven with swirls or areas of broken water.

Overhanging trees, weed rafts or undercut banks when combined with deeper water and a steady flow make classic chub holding areas. Slower water downstream of obstructions such as bushes or trees is also worth exploring.

While chub are generally not fussy about what food they eat and will tolerate quite strong tackle, they do not tolerate disturbance, so after taking one or two chub from a swim, it's time to move on. A quiet roving approach is the key to success when chub fishing on small rivers.

It is often recommended that you walk the river, feeding several likely looking swims before fishing, then fishing each in turn after the chub have had time to find and eat the free offerings.

This definitely works and is a good approach for long sessions, but when fishing time is limited, as mine often is, it is still possible to have a productive session without pre-baiting as long as you approach each swim quietly and do not cause any disturbance before you start fishing.

While I'm not suggesting that you need to tip toe to your swim, or crawl the last few yards on your hands and knees, you do need to approach the swim carefully. Think of it as trying to sneak up unawares behind a wild animal you are hunting.

Stay low and put your tackle and chair down softly. If you are using rod rests, push them into the ground as quietly as you can and keep your movements to a minimum. Position everything near to hand so you can keep as still as possible while fishing.

Introduce a few samples of your hook bait and wait a few minutes before casting in your tackle to give the chub time to find the free offerings and become confident. This is good practice even if you have pre-baited the swim earlier.

Chub will take most baits, but small baits such as maggots and the smaller varieties of worms will often attract the attentions of smaller fish in the swim, so I prefer to use more selective larger baits such as bread, cheese paste and lobworms. On some waters, boilies and large pellets can also be effective.

Of all baits, my favourite for chub fishing is home made cheese paste.

I have caught more large chub on this bait that any other and although that is likely to be as much because of my preference for using it, as its appeal to chub, it is a highly effective chub bait. You will find details of how to make cheese paste and other paste baits in the chapter on baits later in this book.

In terms of tackle, an Avon style rod with a test curve around 1.25lb will be powerful enough to tame quite large chub. While most bites will be positive and pull the tip round, it can be an advantage to use the lightest quivertip that will hold against the flow, as on occasions, bites will only show as gentle plucks or a slight tightening of the line.

Chub are not generally too tackle shy, so a main line of 6lb (2.75kg) and a hook length of 4lb to 5lb (1.8kg to 2.2kg) will usually be fine, but you may need to scale down a little if the river is low and clear.

The end tackle doesn't have to be complicated. A simple link leger rig (below left) will be fine in most swims and is versatile as you can add or remove weight to suit the conditions in each swim you fish. In particularly heavy flows, a simple running leger rig (below right) can be used if you need more weight to hold bottom.

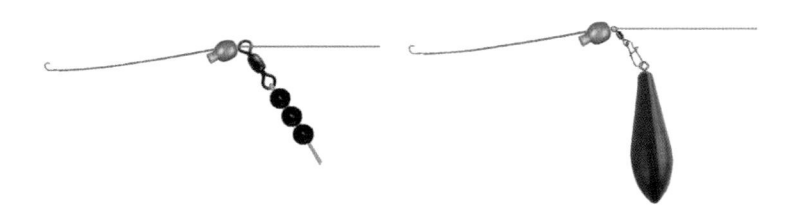

Use the least amount of weight necessary to hold against the flow as this will offer the least resistance to the fish and provide the most sensitive bite detection. It also allows you to gently lift the weight off the bottom and drift the bait with the current from time to time to search through the swim.

Diagrams for construction of link leger and running leger rigs are included in the chapter on leger rigs later in this book.

Hook size should be matched to the size of bait you are using. For worms and bread flake I use a size 12 or 10, stepping up to a size 8 for paste.

If you are using a paste bait, there is no need to leave the hook point showing, if you make the paste soft enough the hook should easily pull through it on the strike.

When casting, try to drop the bait gently into the water without causing a large splash. If you are fishing close to the near bank, you should be able to do this with a careful under arm swing. If casting further, try to cast as gently as you can to minimise disturbance.

Bites can come almost immediately, so although I use a front rest to steady the rod, I usually hold the rod while waiting for a bite with the butt of the rod resting across my knee. To keep the weight needed to hold bottom to a minimum, I angle the rod upwards to keep line off the water.

You will often be fishing in confined swims between trees and bushes so position your rod rests so the rod is pointing a little down stream to give you room for the strike.

If I don't get a bite right away, I will usually fish a swim for 30 to 45 minutes before moving on. I might stay a little longer if I have seen fish activity such as line bites, but it is usually best to maximise your chances by not staying too long in one place and fishing as many swims as possible.

Often the disturbance caused by playing and landing a chub will disturb the swim too much and another chub from the same swim will be unlikely for some time, but it is sometimes possible to get a second if you've been able to get the first one out quite quickly.

Before moving on it pays to put some more samples of your hook bait into the swim so you can try it again later in the session.

You will often be fishing very close to snags such a submerged branches or tree roots and as soon as a chub feels resistance it will head for the nearest snag, so be prepared to bully it until you've stopped the first one or two lunges.

This is one of those occasions when fish can be lost if the clutch on the reel isn't tight. For chub fishing I always fish with the clutch wound down tight and give line by back winding the reel under gentle pressure to make the chub work to gain line.

Sometimes you just have to hold on tight for a few seconds and trust that the hook will stay put until the chub tires and you can guide it away from danger.

Most days, if you are careful and don't cause disturbance, chub will bite boldly. This is especially the case on overcast days and as the sun starts to go down at dusk. On bright days when the water is low and clear, you may need to scale down your tackle and fish very close to snags to tempt a fish.

Increasing the length of line between the weight and hook and fishing with a slack line can also tempt bites on hard days when bites are fickle and difficult to hit.

To summarise, if you travel light, fish quietly and carefully and are prepared to move swims several times in a session, the chub in your river will usually oblige.

TACTICS FOR BARBEL

The barbel is a powerful streamlined fish that is at home in very fast currents. It is primarily a bottom feeder with a low set mouth flanked by barbels that it uses to search for food on the bed of the river.

As the barbel is a specialised bottom feeder, it follows that legering a bait hard on the bottom is the most successful method for catching them and this is certainly the case on large rivers such as the Severn which is famous for its barbel populations in the upper reaches.

Legering is an effective technique in small rivers too, but some small river swims can provide excellent sport for barbel using float fishing tactics.

Barbel fishing calls for strong tackle. Many tackle companies offer a stepped up version of the Avon rod, described as a Barbel Avon with a test curve of 1.5lb to 2.75lb and these are ideal for both float fishing and legering.

Many specialist barbel anglers favour a centrepin reel as it provides more direct contact with the fish, but a fixed spool reel will be fine and the higher retrieve rate of a fixed spool reel over a centrepin can be an advantage if you have to retrieve line quickly when the barbel changes direction and swims upstream towards you.

A main line of at least 6lb (2.75kg) is advisable, along with a strong forged wire hook either tied direct to the main line or to a hook length of a slightly lower breaking strain.

Even relatively small barbel can exert incredible pressure on tackle so check all knots carefully before and during fishing to ensure there are no weak links.

At one time the accepted practice was to introduce a bed of hempseed into the swim and fish over that with a lump of luncheon meat. Another popular method was to feed a mix of hemp and casters with two or three casters on the hook.

In both cases, large quantities of hempseed are introduced into the swim too attract barbel and keep them in the swim searching for the small food items.

In recent years, a pellet approach has become popular, halibut pellets being the preferred bait. of many barbel anglers, but the principle of introducing large quantities of small particles to hold barbel in the swim is the same.

I usually like to prime the swim with bait at the start of the session and add more bait regularly while fishing. If the flow is not too strong, bait can be thrown in by hand, but in more powerful swims, bait is best introduced using a swimfeeder.

Many anglers use a block end feeder with enlarged holes to enable the bait to be washed out by the current, but I prefer to use an open ended feeder, with a stiff groundbait mix used as a carrier for the hempseed or pellets.

My usual groundbait mix consists mainly of brown crumb. If I am using hempseed as loose feed, some of the water in which the hemp was boiled is used to wet the groundbait. If I am using pellets as loose feed, some crushed pellets are added to the dry base mix. before water is added.

In both cases, the scent and flavour of the loose feed is introduced into the water which I believe can draw fish up stream into your swim in search of food.

Once mixed to a stiff consistency, I then add hempseed or pellets into the groundbait and mix well. A small amount of groundbait can carry a large quantity of particles when packed into an open ended swimfeeder, but is easily washed out by the current when the rig lands on the river bed.

For legering, I favour a simple link leger rig, with either a swimfeeder or leger weight that is just heavy enough to hold bottom. Hook size is matched to the size of the hook bait, from size 14 being about right for two or three casters, 12 for a banded pellet, up to size 8 or 6 for luncheon meat.

When fishing with luncheon meat I normally use a short hair rig as it is an awkward bait to cast any distance and I find that a hair rig can help to prevent the meat coming off the hook on the cast.

Barbel bites can be very powerful, so whether you choose to hold the rod, or place it in rests, you should ensure that the rod is close to hand so that you can react as soon as you get a bite. It is not unknown for barbel to pull rods off rests with their initial run and you need to be able to pick up the rod and take control as quickly as possible.

Although legering probably accounts for the vast majority of barbel caught, some swims are more effectively tackled with a float.

Such swims are typically quite shallow from the near bank to three quarters of the way across the river, with a deeper undercut channel under trees along the far bank.

This is a very active form of fishing as the fast current will carry the float to the end of the swim very quickly requiring constant casting and feeding, but if barbel are present in the swim, very good catches are possible.

The flow in such swims is typically very strong, so a float that can carry a lot of shot such as a balsa (below left) or chubber (below right), with the shot bulked near the hook, is needed to get the bait down quickly and moving close to the bottom.

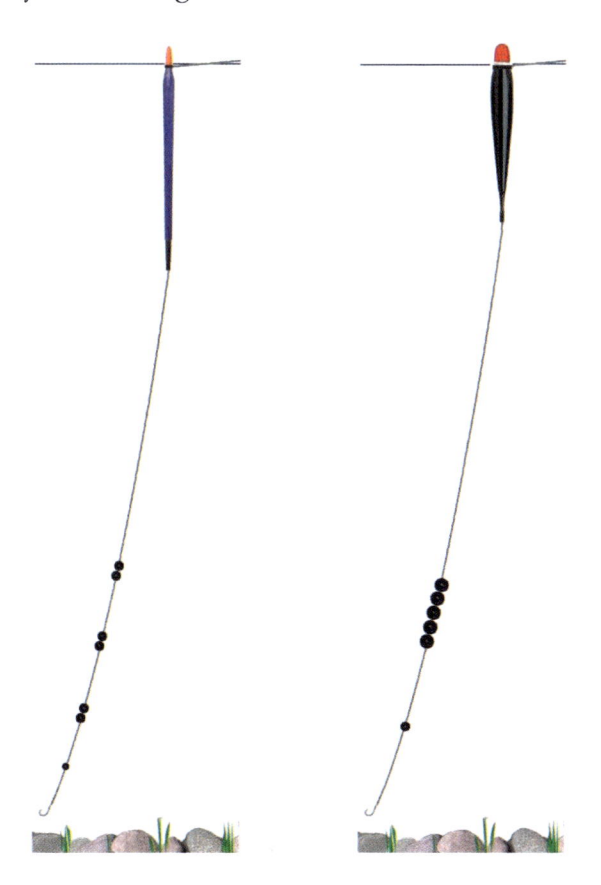

These rigs are explained in more detail in the rigs chapter later in this book.

You will usually need to wade to mid river and fish standing up so you can cast accurately and control the float down the swim. Start by throwing a handful of loose feed a little upstream on the line you intend to fish and swing the tackle into the swim so that it follows the path of the loose feed. It can sometimes pay to slow the float down a little, but usually allowing the float to travel at the speed of the current will produce bites.

A strike is not usually necessary, just a tightening of the line when the float goes under will most times be met by a powerful pull from the barbel as it makes its bid for freedom towards tree roots and other snags under the far bank.

You will need to hold on tight to draw the fish away from far bank snags into clearer water where you can play it safely, but the combination of the barbel's power and streamlined shape with the strong flow of the river rarely makes for a short fight even with relatively small barbel of just a few pounds.

One characteristic of barbel is that they fight to the last and rarely give up until they are completely exhausted. Once landed, it is important that barbel are unhooked quickly and they often need to be held in the water to revive before being released.

I always lower a barbel into the water facing upstream and support it gently until it is ready to swim off. When it is ready, it will power out of your hands with a kick of its tail.

If you want to weigh or photograph a barbel, rest it in the water in your landing net while you get everything ready. If the fish is showing distress, wait until it has recovered before weighing or photographing and rest it again before release.

TACTICS FOR PERCH

Small rivers can contain surprisingly large perch up to several pounds, and over the years I have caught many good specimens.

I have to confess, though, that I rarely set out to target perch specifically, most captures have either been made while fishing for other species, or opportunistically when I have become aware of their presence in the swim I was fishing.

This is not because I don't like to fish for perch, in fact quite the opposite. Perch are game fighters and always welcome, but they are not present in large numbers in the rivers I fish regularly, so I rarely target them to the exclusion of other species.

If you want to specifically target perch on your local river, you will need to spend some time finding out where they are. This is best done early in the day when they are more likely to be active and they will generally be found in or near deeper areas of the river near cover such as lily pads, rushes, bushes and trees.

At this time of day, perch will often be seen attacking shoals of minnows and fry. You may see the distinct dorsal fin of the perch breaking the surface, or see the commotion of small fish and fry jumping out of the water as the perch attack from below.

At other times perch will usually be near cover from which they can ambush passing prey, but they can be in any part of the river. I once caught a perch of almost three pounds on legered maggots in a run of quite fast water less than a foot (30cm) deep.

Good baits for perch are worms, both small and large, bunches of maggots and small freshwater fish, both live and dead. Minnows can work particularly well in small rivers.

Maggots will attract the attention of all fish in the swim, so they are not the best choice of hook bait if you particularly want to catch only perch, but they are a good attractor both of perch and the small fish on which they feed, so feeding maggots while fishing a larger bait such as a lobworm can be very effective.

These days I do not use live bait or kill freshwater fish for bait, so most of my perch fishing is done with worms, either whole or half a lobworm or a bunch of two or three redworms. Perch, unlike pike, will not take sea fish baits of any kind.

If you are happy to use live and/or dead baits, minnows are very effective if they are present in any numbers in the river. Other fish that can be successful include small roach, dace and, perhaps surprisingly, perch, which many experienced anglers believe are the best perch bait of all.

Perch do not grow very large and a fish of 3lb (1.36kg) is a good specimen, so a main line of 3lb to 3.5lb (1.3kg to 1.5kg) should be strong enough for any perch you catch in a small river.

For most of my perch fishing, I use one of three rigs depending on the type of swim I am fishing.

For swims where I can trot a float alongside cover such as a bed of rushes or under a canopy of trees or overhanging bushes, I use a chubber float rig to ease a large worm bait down the swim. This technique is also well suited to trotting with live minnows.

This rig can also double as a float leger rig in slow and slack water by fishing it over depth with the shot resting on the bottom.

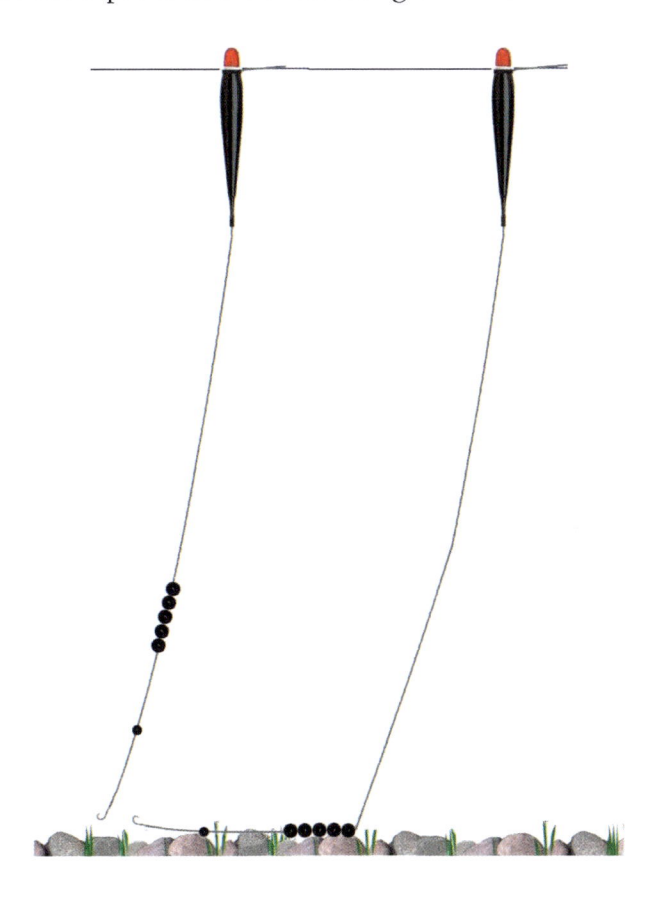

When trotting a reasonably fast swim, bites are usually positive demanding a quick strike, but when float legering, the float will often dip slightly, lift out of the water or move a little sideways, sometimes for several seconds or even over a minute before the perch takes the bait properly causing the float to slide away.

This is very similar to the fussy bites that are typical of tench in still waters and it is important to wait for a positive indication before striking if you are to connect with the perch.

In faster water in swims that are not suitable for trotting I switch to a simple link leger or sliding leger rig, choosing one or the other depending on how much weight is required for the rig to just hold bottom in the current.

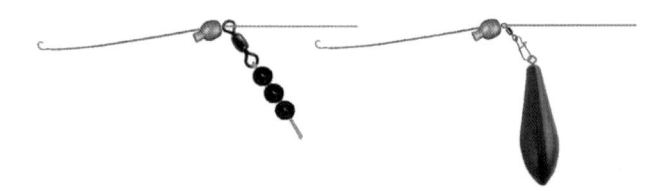

A fine rod tip or sensitive quivertip is required for this style of fishing. While smaller perch will often pull the tip round sharply once or twice before taking the bait properly, larger perch can cause the tip to twitch for an extended period, much like they do when you are float legering, before giving a positive indication that you can strike.

In quite shallow water of a foot or two ((30cm to 60cm) I prefer to use a simple freeline rig with no weight on the line to avoid the splash of a weight entering the water disturbing the fish.

The only practical bait for this style of fishing, unless you do not have to cast any distance at all, is a large lobworm or minnow which provides enough casting weight but will enter the water softly.

A slack line from the hook to rod tip is required for this type of fishing so the perch feels no resistance when taking the worm. Bites, as with float legering, may begin with a few light plucks before a positive tightening of the line signals the time to strike.

A bite can sometimes be induced by gently twitching the bait to impart movement or to move it an inch or two across the bottom from time to time.

On overcast days or in areas of shade, large perch may feed throughout the day so if you think they may be perch about, hedging your bets by fishing a large worm bait will give you a chance of catching perch, while still giving you a chance of a good chub or roach.

If you see signs that perch are actively hunting, they can sometimes be caught using a small spinner, but for this method to be viable you need plenty of room both for casting and for working the spinner through the water.

If you want to try spinning, small patterns of the Mepps type of spinner are generally considered to be good for perch.

You should use a wire trace when spinning as although perch cannot bite through line, there will often be pike present in the river.

TACTICS FOR PIKE

If you spend time fishing a river, you will soon get to know if it contains a lot of pike. On days when you are happily catching roach and dace on the float, they will often make their presence known by grabbing a fish as you are winding it in.

If you want to fish for pike, they are usually easy to find. When they are not actively hunting out in the stream they generally prefer quiet water and will be found where the river is wide and slow, in back eddies and the slower water on bends.

Pike like cover from which they can ambush their prey, so undercut banks, weed beds and deep water beneath trees and bushes are reliable places to try.

Tackle for large pike needs to be stronger than that used for other species, but for fish up to low double figures, an Avon rod suitable for barbel fishing with a test curve of about 1.75lb will be powerful enough.

If your river contains larger pike, a more specialist rod with a test curve of 2.5lb would be a better choice.

Line strength should be stepped up too. Pike are not generally bothered by strong tackle, so use a main line of 10lb to 12lb and always use a wire trace.

Ready made pike traces incorporating one or two treble hooks are easily available from tackle shops so there is no need to make your own.

If you can, get them without barbs, or with only one hook of the treble barbed to hold the bait. If you can only get traces with barbed hooks, flatten or file off the barbs before fishing.

Having two treble hooks inside a pike's mouth or throat, making up to six individual hooks to deal with, is bad enough when they are barbless. Unless you are experienced at unhooking pike, barbed trebles add unnecessary difficulty to unhooking pike on uneven river banks.

Personally, I no longer use treble hooks for small river pike fishing. Several years ago I switched to using a single large barbless hook and I don't believe it has resulted in me missing more bites or losing more fish than when I was using trebles.

It is important to keep a tight line while playing a pike on a single barbless hook as it not hold as firmly as multiple trebles, but I don't find this a problem and unhooking pike is much easier.

Whether to use single or treble hooks is up to personal choice, but if you are inexperienced at unhooking pike I urge you to use single hooks or barbless trebles for the sake of the pike. It may be a fearsome predator in the water, but on the bank it is surprisingly fragile and needs to be returned to the water as quickly as possible.

Terminal tackle for pike fishing has already been covered in the chapter on tackle, so the rest of this chapter will cover some basic small river pike fishing techniques.

I have included diagrams and instructions for the construction of several popular pike set ups in the rigs chapter later in this book, but I use the inline float rig for most of my small river pike fishing.

Although primarily designed as a running water float rig, it can also be used to suspend a static bait in still and slow moving areas and by increasing the depth of the rig so all of the shot is resting on the bottom, adding more shot if necessary, it can be used as a float leger rig.

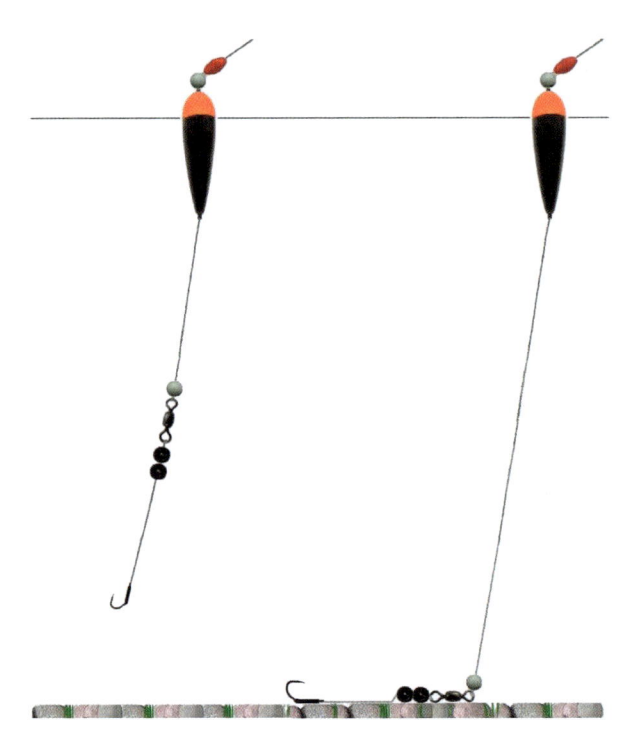

As with most small river fishing, pike fishing is a roving method, so using a rig that is flexible enough to be used in a variety of swims and conditions saves a lot of time that would otherwise be spent changing rigs with each move of swim.

With the exception of lure fishing, that I will cover later in this chapter, I use either sprats or sardines for all of my small river pike fishing.

I prefer not to use live baits, but on some waters they will catch more pike than dead baits so if they are allowed on the waters you intend to fish, whether to use them or not is your personal choice.

The method that I will use in a particular swim is dictated by the conditions.

On swims where trotting is possible, preferably in reasonably deep water along the near bank, I will start by trotting a small sprat about a foot (30cm) off the bottom. If I don't get bites after a few trots through, I will try different depths until I get a bite or move to another swim.

I prefer to use small sprats when trotting for two reasons. Firstly, they are similar in size and appearance to small roach and dace which the pike will be used to feeding on. Secondly, they are small so the pike should be able to take the whole fish and hook into its mouth and I can strike as soon as the float goes under, being reasonably confident that I will hook the pike.

If the water on the near bank is quite shallow I use the same trotting technique in the deeper water further out in the river, but if there is slow water of a reasonable depth on the inside bank I will usually try legering either with a sprat or all or part of a sardine in the slower water first, as pike will often be resting there, especially if there is cover.

Pike have longer to inspect and take a static bait than one that is moving down the river, so while the first indication that you get of a bite may be a run as the pike picks up the bait and swims off, very often you will see other signs first, such as bubbles appearing around the float, or the float bobbing or moving slightly.

Sometimes these come to nothing, but if the pike takes the bait you should see the float go under or move quickly across the water. Both are indications that you should strike immediately. If you wait, the pike may have time to swallow the bait and hook(s) which you should always try to avoid.

For swims where the inline float rig is not suitable for fishing a static bait, such as those where there is thick weed on the bottom of the river, I use the paternoster float leger rig which allows a static bait to be suspended above the weed. If there is enough flow to give lifelike movement to the bait, a small sprat suspended above the bottom is a good imitation of a struggling or injured fish which pike will often find irresistible.

This is also a good rig to drop quietly into near bank holes on arriving at a swim and will often result in an immediate take.

There are days when small pike of a few pounds ((known as jacks) will chase and attack anything that moves. On such days I have hooked them when retrieving a large lump of cheese paste intended for chub.

The pike wasn't interested in the cheese paste, it simply reacted to what appeared to be a potential food item that appeared to be swimming past. On such days they will also chase small roach and dace that you have hooked and are winding in.

Even if I don't intend to fish for pike, I carry a small selection of lures so that I can catch any nuisance pike that turn up in the swim and return them to the river a few yards downstream.

It is a simple matter to remove the rig I am using, tie a wire trace to the line and clip on a small spinner or jelly lure. It can be a lot of fun playing a small pike of 5lb or so on relatively light tackle and if the pike are particularly active in the river, I sometimes abandon the roach or chub fishing and spend a few hours spinning for pike.

You should take care when unhooking pike. Not just because they have a mouth full of sharp teeth, but because they are quite fragile out of water.

Always use an unhooking mat to protect the pike if it thrashes about during unhooking and use forceps or pliers to grip the shank of the hook(s) and remove them as quickly as possible.

If the pike's mouth is closed, inserting a finger into the gill and gently lifting the pike's head will cause the lower jaw to open. If you do not feel comfortable doing this, wear an unhooking glove and gently pull the mouth open using the tip of the lower jaw.

Barbless hooks should come out easily with gentle pressure. If the hooks are too far down the pike's throat for you to reach, gently pull on the trace to draw them closer.

After unhooking the pike should be gently lowered into the river near the bank and supported until it swims away. On uneven and hard banks, carrying the pike to the water in the landing net is safer than carrying it in your hands.

FUN WITH GUDGEON AND MINNOWS

The larger fish covered in earlier chapters often share their river with shoals of gudgeon and minnows and if you're trying to target the larger species, especially if you're trotting a glide for roach or dace with maggots, these smaller fish can be a frustrating nuisance.

They can be a lot of fun too though. If you just want to spend a couple of hours on the river unwinding after a day at work, or you want to save a blank at the end of a day when big fish tactics haven't brought any results, gudgeon and minnows will usually oblige.

Tackle doesn't have to be anything fancy, just a stick float shotted shirt button style, or with the shot bunched in the bottom half of the line for short fast runs. A size 16 or 18 hook and 2lb to 2.5lb hook length finishes the rig, with single maggot on the hook.

This is one of those occasions where stealth isn't necessary, but it can still pay to be quiet and careful as there may be some better fish such as roach or perch in the swim and feeding half a dozen maggots each cast may get them interested.

Swims with a slacker area just off the main flow are best. Gudgeon seem to like back eddies where the current swirls back on itself and allowing the float to work around with the current, however wrong it might look, is usually all you need to do to catch a few.

Introduce a few samples of your hook bait each cast and allow the float to work around the swim while holding the rod. Bites are rarely fickle, usually the float will dive sharply under the surface and all that is needed is a firm strike to hook the fish.

Be prepared to give line if you hook something bigger. By introducing loose feed regularly you can often attract the attention of larger fish such as roach and perch.

JUNGLE SWIMS

Many streams and the upper reaches of rivers are very overgrown with trees hanging over the banks.

If you poke your head through the trees you will often see areas of reasonable depth with classic fish holding features such as an overhanging bush or tree roots growing into the water, but fishing these jungle swims is impossible with even the 10ft rod I use for most of my small river fishing.

I used to pass these areas by although I did often have a look through the bushes on my way past. Several times I saw fish, chub and perch mostly, but even if I could have got a bait to them, playing them in such a confined space would have been impossible.

Often there was a canopy of tree above the swim and if I tried to lift the rod to play the fish, either I wouldn't be able to lift it high enough, or more likely, the line would have tangled among the branches.

One solution would have been to take a short spinning rod of 6ft to 7ft for these swims, but I try to keep the tackle I carry to a minimum, so the solution I came up with was to make a short handle that would fit into the middle section of my 3 piece 10ft river rod, giving me a fishable length of a little over 7ft.

This isn't a new idea, short handle sections to allow a rod to be used at more than one length were popular many years ago, the short handle being known as a dolly butt.

At this length, the rod doesn't have the power it has at it's full length so playing fish of a few pounds in such a confined space can be a little hair raising. Usually I have to hold on tight to stop the fish reaching a snag, trusting that the tackle will hold, while the rod bends into an alarming hoop, but it is a lot of fun.

Fish in these overgrown swims are not usually tackle shy as they feel safe, so fairly strong tackle can be used, which is just as well as it needs to be. You will often be hooking the fish no more than a couple of feet from a snag and they will try to reach it as soon as they are hooked.

A simple link leger or small bomb rig can be used, but for the tightest swims, to keep everything as simple as possible I often just tie a size 8 or 10 hook directly to the main line and attach one or two SSG shot four to six inches from the hook.

I find the best bait for this type of fishing is a large worm, either a whole dendrobaena or half a lobworm. Worms are a completely natural bait and can often produce a bite straight away without the need to introduce free samples to get the fish feeding.

Positioning the bait in the swim can be a little tricky as there's no room to cast. Sometimes you can just poke the rod above the water and lower the bait in under the rod tip, but usually its necessary to use a gentle well timed pendulum swing to flick the bait a few feet from the bank.

Once the bait is in the water a bite could come at any time, so hold on to the rod and stay alert. A bite often shows as no more than a tightening of the line as the fish starts to move away, so be ready to strike and hold on tight!

FISHING IN FLOOD CONDITIONS

Rivers usually fish best when they are fining down after a flood. There is still a tinge of colour in the water that helps to hide you from the fish and increases their confidence. A lot of natural food such as worms and grubs will have been washed into the water stimulating the fish to feed.

For most anglers though, who can only fish at weekends, it is not always possible to fish when the river is at its best and sometimes fishing while the river is still high is unavoidable.

Much of the river will be unfishable due to strong flows and boily or broken water which is too heavy for both tackle and fish, but the fish are still in the river and if they can be found they can still be caught.

The first step is to find a swim where the current is less strong, providing a comfortable area for fish to wait out the flood.

Look for swims near the bank where a slacker area is created by trees or bushes in the water. The insides of bends often contain slack water out of the main flow and the mouths of small streams and ditches where they enter the river are worth exploring too.

Not all slack areas will contain fish, so you may need to adopt a roving approach and fish several swims during a session until you find a fish holding area.

If you can't find an area of slack water, look for swims where there is a stretch of water that is out of the main flow and where the surface is steady without boils or broken water.

The fish have to be somewhere and barbel, in particular, will tolerate quite strong flows, taking advantage of the extra food being washed down by the flood.

Strong tackle is needed in these conditions. An Avon rod with a test curve of 1.5lb to 1.75lb will help you to combat the extra flow and bully fish away from snags.

Line of at least 6lb (2.75kg) should be used. In extreme conditions where large fish are present, step up to 8lb (3.6kg) or more and use strong forged wire hooks.

While you may be able to use float rigs in the slackest swims, most will call for a legering approach using much heavier leger weights than usual to hold against the stronger flow.

Due to the amount of dislodged weed and other debris in the water, a simple running leger or feeder rig is best in flood conditions.

A simple streamlined rig will present less resistance to the current and minimise build up of weed on the line.

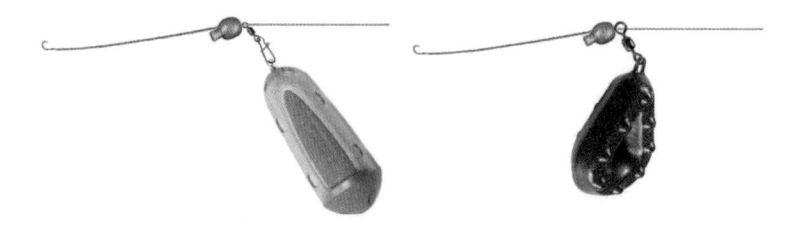

Flat leads will hold better than streamlined pear shaped leads against a strong current, but in extreme conditions you may need to use a large gripper lead to hold bottom.

Fish will be feeding less by sight and more by smell in the low visibility conditions, so luncheon meat flavoured with curry powder or strong cheese paste baits will be more easily found by the fish.

Worms are also an excellent bait in flood conditions. Some scent will be released where the hook enters the worm, but to maximise the amount of scent I prefer to use large lobworms cut in half, using one or both halves on the hook.

You will get many plucks and pulls on the rod tip when fishing in floods. Some of these are fish, but many will be caused by debris catching on the line. Large baits are not easily pulled off a hook, so wait for a strong definite bite before striking.

If you are getting a lot of false bites caused by debris striking the line, or a build up of weed is masking the hook or pulling the rig out of position, casting upstream should reduce the problem as weed and other debris will slide away from the leger and hook.

When casting upstream, tighten up to the leger and bites will show as a slackening of the line as the leger is disturbed and drops down the river towards you.

Although the water will be heavily coloured and hiding you from the fish, a quiet and careful approach is still necessary as any vibration will be transmitted into the water and disturb fish which may be only inches from the bank.

While fishing a river in flood can be rewarding, it can also be dangerous. The ground will be slippery underfoot so take care when approaching the water.

Banks that have been undercut by strong flooding may collapse under your weight and if the river is still rising, your route back to the car may be cut off by deep water in flooded fields.

Fishing in flood conditions and wading across flooded fields is not advisable on waters that you do not know well, so stick to waters you know, fish with a friend if possible and take extra care.

A LESS SELECTIVE APPROACH

In previous chapters I have described methods for targeting particular species of fish, but if you have read this far you will, no doubt, have noticed that tactics for many species are quite similar.

For example, when targeting large roach with bread flake you may well catch a chub and if you fish with maggots or small worms you could catch a fish of almost any size or species.

To me, this is one of the main attractions of small river fishing. By using methods and baits that will work for a variety of species you could, quite literally, catch a small gudgeon on one cast followed by a 3lb chub on the next.

By all means, if you want to target a particular species, use a method and bait that is most likely to give you the result you want, but if you are content to simply catch fish it pays to take a more generalist approach.

There are occasions when I particularly want to target large specimens of a single species. I may have spotted some large roach on a previous trip to the river, so I will fish with a large piece of bread flake in the knowledge that although I may still catch a sizeable chub or possibly dace, my chances of catching a roach are increased.

Similarly, if I believe large perch are in the vicinity, I will fish with large lobworms. Again, I could catch another species such as a chub or barbel if they are present, but by using a bait that I know will be taken readily by perch, my chances of catching one are improved.

Most of the time, though, I am content to simply catch fish and I will often use small baits such as maggots or redworms to maximise my chances.

If I am catching a lot of small fish, but sense that there are larger fish in the swim, I can always try a larger or more selective bait for half an hour to see if I can attract something bigger.

I have heard it said that if you want to catch large fish, there are really only two ways to go about it; fish selectively with large baits so you only catch large fish, or catch as many fish as you can and some of them will be large.

My approach is usually the latter, especially if I can find a swim that is suited to trotting a float. This, by far, is my favourite style of fishing. You literally do not know, from one trot through the swim to the next, what might take your bait.

For me, there is little that can beat the thrill of striking a slight dip of the float expecting another 3oz roach, only to be shocked into action by something much larger pulling on the other end of the line!

As I mentioned in the chapter on pike, I also take a small amount of pike tackle and spinners so that I am equipped to take advantage on days when the pike are active. A pike of 5lb or so is a small specimen for a pike, but it's still a good sized fish for a river and is fun to catch.

Small rivers may not offer the almost guaranteed results that you can get on carp stocked stillwaters and on some days they can be really frustrating, but if you enjoy a challenge in surroundings shaped by nature, a day spent on a river could give you the most enjoyable day's fishing you've ever had.

SMALL RIVER TECHNIQUES AND RIGS

You only need to master a few simple techniques and rigs for small river fishing, but they are quite different to those you will be used to if you have only fished stillwaters.

This chapter contains an explanation of techniques and rigs for river fishing that I have mentioned in earlier chapters.

Small river fishing often means adopting a mobile approach and fishing several swims during a session. As each swim often requires a different tactic or rig than the last, I find it convenient to have several different rigs already made up on winders so I don't have to set up a new rig from scratch when I change swim.

FLOAT FISHING TECHNIQUES AND RIGS

When float fishing on rivers you will usually attach the float to the line using silicon or plastic tubing placed at both ends of the float. This is known as 'top and bottom' or 'double rubber'.

Shot is then attached to the line between the float and the hook, either spaced out or in bunches so that only the tip of the float is visible above the water.

As the float will move with the current you need to continually pay out line, so the bale arm of the reel is left open and the line is controlled by pressure applied with your finger at the edge of the spool.

To keep a tight line to the float you may need to 'mend the line' by trapping the line with your finger and lifting the rod until the line between the rod tip and float is straight. On rivers where there are many surface currents you may need to do this several times on each passage of the float down the swim.

Although fishing at the speed of the current will usually work well, it can sometimes pay to slow the float down slightly by releasing line under gentle tension so that it moves at slightly less than the speed of the current.

Bites can sometimes be induced by holding back the float momentarily so that the hook bait lifts off the bottom. This can be particularly effective if done at the end of the swim before reeling in to make the next cast.

STICK FLOAT RIG

The basic stick float rig is suitable for medium paced rivers.

The float is attached to the line using two pieces of silicon tubing. For wire stemmed stick floats a third piece of tubing is used at the base of the balsa body.

The shot required to set the float is made up of several shots, size 4, 6 or 8 depending on the capacity of the float, spaced evenly down the line.

The float should be allowed to travel through the swim at the speed of the current. Mend the line as necessary to keep a straight line to the float so it is not dragged or pulled out of position by the current.

Bites can sometimes be induced by holding back the float momentarily from time to time so the bait lifts in the water.

Shotting can be adjusted by bunching the shots together if a slower or faster falling bait is required by conditions on the day.

BALSA FLOAT RIG

The balsa float rig is suitable for fast flowing rivers.

The float is attached to the line using two pieces of silicon tubing.

The shot required to set the float is made up of bunches of shots spaced evenly down the lower half of the line. Depending on the shot capacity of the float and the speed of the current, quite large shots, up to number 1 or BB may be required.

For very fast flows where the fish are feeding very close to the bottom, it may be necessary to bunch all of the shots together a few inches above the dropper shot.

The float should be controlled through the swim usually at the speed of the current, but it can sometimes be effective to release line under tension so the float travels slightly slower.

Mend the line as necessary to keep a straight line to the float so it is not dragged or pulled out of position by the current.

AVON FLOAT RIG

The Avon float rig is suitable for fishing at close range in rivers with a medium to fast flow.

The float is attached to the line using three pieces of silicon tubing placed at the top and bottom of the float and just below the body.

Shotting consists of a bunch of large shot, AAA or BB depending on the shotting capacity of the float about 2 feet (30cm) from the hook, and a smaller dropper shot.

On entering the water, the bulk of large shot will quickly take the hook bait to the bottom and the float is them allowed to move through the swim at the speed of the current.

Mend the line as necessary to keep a straight line to the float so it is not dragged or pulled out of position by the current.

Bites can sometimes be induced by slowing down the float or holding it back momentarily from time to time so the bait lifts in the water.

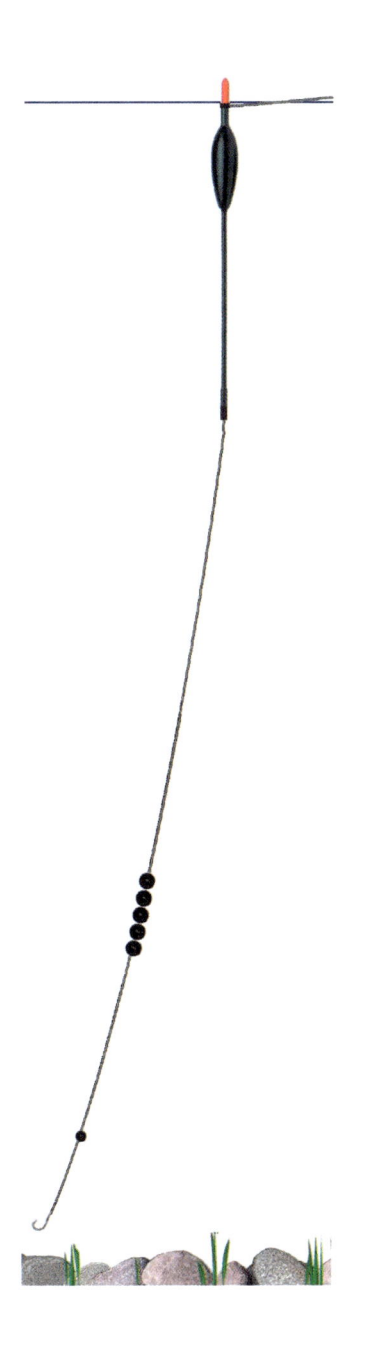

CHUBBER FLOAT RIG

The chubber float rig is suitable for fishing fast flowing shallow rivers with large baits such as worms and bread.

The float is attached to the line using two pieces of silicon tubing.

The shot required to set the float is made up of a single bunch of large shot, AAA or SSG depending on the shot carrying capacity of the float, with a single dropper, number 4 or number 6, near the hook.

The float should be controlled through the swim usually at the speed of the current, but it can sometimes be effective to release line under tension so the float travels slightly slower.

Mend the line as necessary to keep a straight line to the float so it is not dragged or pulled out of position by the current.

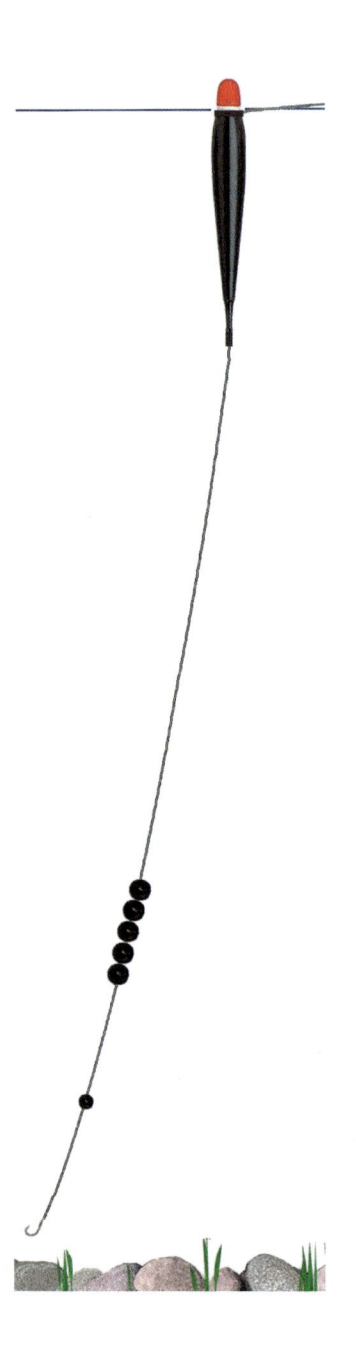

LEGERING TECHNIQUES AND RIGS

When river fishing, although casting weight is a factor, you should use the lightest leger weight or swimfeeder that will just hold bottom against the current.

A bite is detected by watching for movement of the rod tip or slackening of the line when a fish takes the bait. Bites may also be detected by holding the line between finger and thumb.

When constructing rigs make sure they will not be a danger to fish in the event of the line breaking. In particular ensure that wherever a break occurs the leger weight or feeder will not remain attached to the hook link.

You may see rig diagrams on the internet for feeder rigs where the feeder is running inside a loop or paternoster rigs where the hook link is tied directly to the main line.

While these were a popular and successful methods in the past, they are not safe rigs as a break in the line above the leger or feeder would leave it attached to a hooked fish.

LINK LEGER RIG

The link leger rig is a versatile rig designed to be used on rivers where there are overhanging trees, snags and rafts of weed.

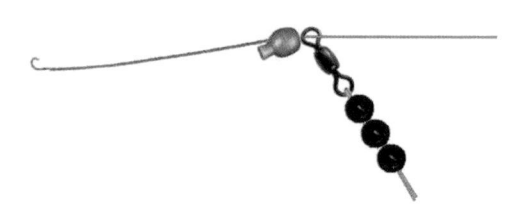

To construct the rig, slide a swivel on to the main line followed by a leger stop (a small split shot or swivel and bead can be used if you prefer), tie a loop in the main line and attach a hook link of 18 inches (45cm).

The weight for this rig is added by passing a short length of line through the eye of the swivel, folding it to form a loop and attaching shot to lock it in place.

You should only add as much shot as is needed to just hold bottom against the current and if conditions change or you move swim you should adjust the shot accordingly.

This rig can be fished like a standard running leger rig, but if no bites are forthcoming, gently raising the rod to disturb the rig will lift it off the bottom and allow you to search the swim by drifting the rig further downstream or under overhanging branches.

FREE-LINING LEGER RIG

Free-lining can be an effective technique when fishing large baits in confined swims.

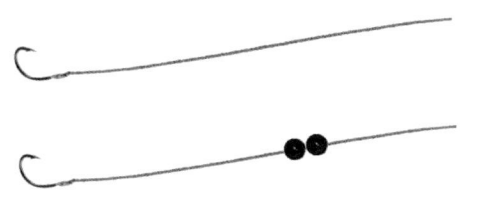

Tie a size 8 or 10 hook directly to the main line. If extra weight is needed, one or two SSG shot can be added 4 to 6 inches from the hook.

Like the link leger rig, this can be fished static on the bottom, or used to search the swim by lifting the rig and allowing it to drift downstream.

RUNNING LEGER/FEEDER RIG

The running leger rig can be used with a leger or swimfeeder.

To construct the rig, slide a link swivel on to the main line followed by a leger stop (a small split shot or swivel and bead can be used if you prefer), tie a loop in the main line and attach a hook link of 18 inches (45cm).

A leger weight or swimfeeder is attached to the rig using the link swivel which gives you the flexibility to switch between leger or feeder, or change to a heavier or lighter leger weight without having to break the rig down.

As the line can pass freely through the eye of the swivel there is little resistance when a fish takes the bait.

SEMI-FIXED LEGER/FEEDER RIG

This is a semi-fixed version of the running leger rig. It can be very effective when bites are difficult to see because the fish are not moving far after taking your bait.

To construct the rig, slide one or two float stops on to the main line, followed by a link swivel and a leger stop (a small split shot or swivel and bead can be used if you prefer), tie a loop in the main line and attach a hook link of 18 inches (45cm).

This rig is designed to provide resistance as soon as a fish takes the bait causing it to either swim away quickly and provide a positive indication of a bite, or hook itself against the weight of the leger or swimfeeder.

PATERNOSTER FEEDER RIG

This is a very sensitive rig that shows up bites very well as any movement of the hook is quickly transmitted up the line to the rod tip.

To construct the rig, slide one or two float stops on to the main line followed by swivel and a soft bead. Tie another swivel to the end of the main line and attach 10 inches (25cm) of line to the other end of the swivel.

The leger or swimfeeder is tied to the end of this line and an 18 inch (45cm) hook link is attached to the swivel between the bead and the float stop. Use the float stop to lock the hook length swivel in place.

You should experiment with longer or shorter hook links if you have difficulty seeing or hitting bites.

RIGS FOR LIVE AND DEAD BAIT FISHING

Live and dead baits are effective for catching pike in small rivers and small live baits such as minnows can be deadly for large perch.

A wire trace is essential when pike fishing as pike have many sharp teeth that can easily cut through fishing line. You should also use a wire trace when targeting perch if there are pike in the river.

This chapter describes popular float and leger rigs for pike and perch fishing that have proven to be effective for small river fishing.

HOW TO HOOK DEAD BAITS

Dead baits are usually attached using a wire trace with two sets of treble hooks, one located at the end of the trace, the other set a short distance back.

The treble hook that is located along the trace should be pushed firmly into the tail root of the dead bait as this hook will bear the force of the cast.

The treble hook positioned at the end of the trace should be lightly hooked into the flesh on the back or side of the dead bait.

If you are using rigs with semi-barbed treble hooks, i.e. two of the points are barbless, insert the barbed points into the dead bait as these will grip the bait much more firmly.

HOW TO HOOK LIVEBAITS

In recent years live baiting has become a controversial subject with some clubs and fisheries banning their use and others imposing rules controlling which rigs can be used.

Where it is allowed, live baits can be hooked in the same way as dead baits using a wire trace with two treble hooks.

An alternative is to use a wire trace terminated by one treble hook and hooking the live bait through one lip using one hook of the treble.

If treble hooks are not allowed on the water you intend to fish, the live bait can be hooked through one lip using a large single hook attached to a wire trace. A single hook is also preferable when fishing small live baits to target perch.

Before using live baits or any of these rigs, check the rules for the river you intend to fish to make sure that they are allowed.

INLINE FLOAT RIG

This versatile rig can be used with both live and dead baits.

To construct the rig, slide a float stop on to the main line (omit this step if you prefer to use a stop knot), followed by a rig bead, then slide on the float followed by another rig bead.

Tie the end of the main line to a pike trace of 2 feet (60cm) in length and attach enough SSG shot at the top of the trace to cock the float.

Use less shot to allow for the weight of the bait if you intend to fish with the bait suspended off the bottom.

This rig can be fished on or above the bottom to drift or move with the current or with the float set over depth to present a semi-static bait on still and slow moving water.

PENCIL SLIDER FLOAT LEGER RIG

This rig works well for legering a dead bait.

To construct the rig, slide a float stop on to the main line (omit this step if you prefer to use a stop knot), followed by a rig bead, then slide on the float followed by another rig bead.

Tie the end of the main line to a pike trace of 2 feet (60cm) in length and attach enough SSG shot at the top of the trace to anchor the bait.

PATERNOSTER FLOAT LEGER RIG

This rig can be used to suspend a bait off the bottom or on top of a bed of weed or sit.

To construct the rig, slide a float stop on to the main line (omit this step if you prefer to use a stop knot), followed by a rig bead, then slide on the float followed by another rig bead.

Tie the end of the main line to a swivel and attach a length of line suitable for the depth at which you want to suspend the bait to the other ring of the swivel.

To complete the rig, attach a pike trace to the top eye using a link swivel.

Use line weaker than the main line with overhand knots tied in it for the leger link. This is often referred to as a 'rotten bottom'.

The leger will break off if it becomes snagged while playing a fish and allows the fish to lose the lead if the line breaks above the swivel.

PATERNOSTER LEGER RIG

This rig can be used to suspend a bait off the bottom or on top of a bed of weed or sit.

To construct the rig, slide a swivel on to the main line, followed by a bead and tie the end of the main line to a pike trace.

Attach a length of line suitable for the depth at which you want to suspend the bait to the other ring of the swivel, attach a foam bait suspender (known as poppers and polyballs) to this line and tie a leger to the other end.

There is no risk of the fish being attached to the leger in the event of a break, but if a weaker line is used for the leger link it will break off if it becomes snagged when playing a fish.

POPPED UP LEGER RIG

This rig can be used to fish a bait off the bottom.

To construct the rig, slide a swivel on to the main line, followed by a bead and tie the end of the main line to a pike trace with bait suspenders (known as poppers and polyballs) attached to suspend the bait.

Attach 2 feet (60cm) of to the other ring of the swivel and tie a leger to the other end.

There is no risk of the fish being attached to the leger in the event of a break, but if a weaker line is used for the leger link it will break off if it becomes snagged when playing a fish.

SIMPLE SINGLE HOOK PIKE TRACE

As I explained in the chapter on pike fishing, I prefer to use single hook rigs rather than trebles when fishing for pike in small rivers.

While there is theoretically more risk of missing bites or losing pike, this has not been the case in my experience and unhooking pike is much easier.

Single hook pike traces are not generally available, but they are easy to construct using wire traces made for spinning, a large eyed hook and a piece of silicon tubing.

I use a hook from size 6 to 2 depending on the pattern.

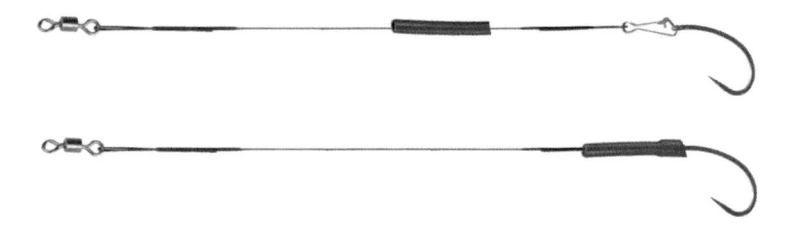

Start with a trace that has a swivel at one end and a snap link or link swivel at the other. Slide a piece of silicon tubing on to the trace, attach the hook to the trace using the snap link and slide the silicon tubing down and over the eye of the hook as shown.

For a more streamlined trace you could substitute heat shrink tubing for the silicon tubing and heat it to shrink it on to the trace.

USEFUL KNOTS

There are many knots that are suitable for fishing, but you need only learn a few to be prepared for any fishing situation.

The two knots below are easy to tie and are suitable for making loops in line.

SURGEON'S LOOP KNOT

Double over the line to form a loop. Form a second loop and pass the doubled end of the line through the second loop three times. Moisten, pull tight and trim.

STEP 1   STEP 2   STEP 3

BLOOD LOOP KNOT

Double over the line to form a loop. Twist the loop and pass the doubled end of the line back through the first loop as shown in step 2 below. Moisten, pull tight and trim.

STEP 1   STEP 2   STEP 3

KNOTS FOR JOINING LINE

The knots in this chapter are used for joining line such as the main line to a hook link.

LOOP METHOD

The simplest method of joining two lengths of line is to use two loops tied using either the surgeon's loop knot or a blood loop knot.

Thread the loops together as shown in step 1 below and pull tight.

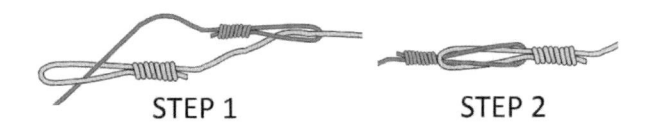

STEP 1   STEP 2

BLOOD KNOT

The blood knot is used to joint lines of similar diameter.

Wrap one length of line around another to form interlocked loops. Twist both loops and pass the standing ends back through the loops where they connect. Pass the standing ends through each of the loops. Moisten, pull tight and trim.

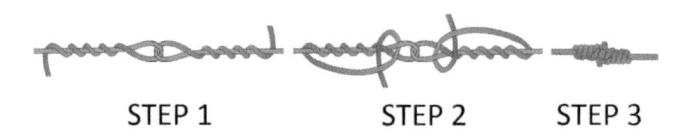

STEP 1   STEP 2   STEP 3

ALBRIGHT KNOT

The Albright knot is used to join lines that are not of similar diameter.

Form a loop in the thicker of the two lines. Pass the end of the thinner line through the loop and wrap it neatly around itself and the loop ten times. Pass the end back through the loop so it exits on the same side it entered. Moisten, pull tight and trim.

STEP 1   STEP 2   STEP 3   STEP 4

KNOTS FOR ATTACHING HOOKS AND SWIVELS

Hooks and swivels can be attached to the line using the knots illustrated below.

SNELL KNOT

This knot can be used to tie either eyed or spade end hooks. If you are tying an eyed hook, first pass the line through the eye of the hook.

Hold the line parallel to the hook shank, form a loop and pass the standing end of the line through the loop five or six times. Moisten, pull tight and trim.

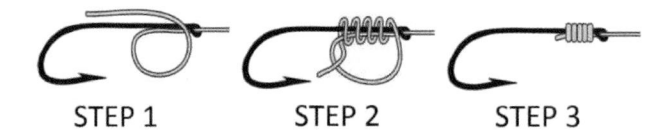

TUCKED HALF BLOOD KNOT

The tucked half blood knot can be used to attach eyed hooks and swivels to line.

Pass the line through the eye of the hook or swivel and twist the line as shown in step 1. Twist the loop and pass the standing end of the line back through the loop next to the eye. Pass the standing end of the line through the loop just created. Moisten, pull tight and trim.

THE KNOTLESS KNOT FOR TYING HAIR RIGS

You can buy hair rigs already tied, but it is very easy to make your own using the knotless knot.

The basic hair rig incorporates a loop that is pulled through a bait, such as a boilie, using a baiting needle and locked in place using a bait stop.

To build on the basic form, you can incorporate additional components into the loop such as maggot clips, boilie spikes and bait bands.

TYING THE KNOTLESS KNOT

Tie a loop for the hair. If you want to include a bait band or boilie spike tie it inside the loop.

Pass the free end of the line through the eye of the hook and pull the line through until you have the length of hair you want, taking into account that if you are using a bait band or boilie spike, the bait will sit off the end of the hair whereas a bait secured with a bait stop have part of the hair inside it.

Wrap the free end of the line back down the hook 8 to 10 times.

Finally, take the free end of the line back to the eye of the hook, pass it back through the eye and pull tight.

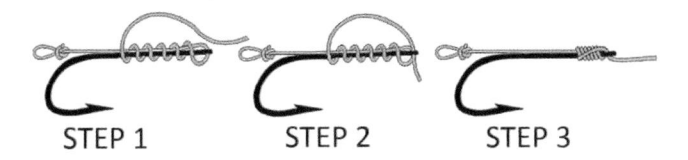

STEP 1   STEP 2   STEP 3

STOP KNOT

Hold the stop knot material to be used for the stop knot (e.g. line or powergum) parallel to the main line. Fold the stop knot material to form a loop and wrap five turns around both the stop knot material and main line inside the loop you have created. Moisten and pull tight.

STEP 1   STEP 2   STEP 3

ARBOR KNOT

The arbor knot is used to attach line or backing to a reel.

Pass the line or backing around the spool and tie an overhand knot around the free end of the line. Tie a second overhand knot in the free end of the line to act as a stop. Slide the knots down to the spool and pull tight.

STEP 1   STEP 2   STEP 3

BAITS FOR SMALL RIVER FISHING

MAGGOTS

Maggots, at one time the most popular bait with match and pleasure anglers, are an excellent small river bait and will often produce bites on the first cast into the swim.

For assessing the fish population of a new river, or amassing a mixed bag of fish of a variety of sizes and species, maggots are hard to beat.

Maggots are not a selective bait and will attract bites from fish of all sizes and species which can be a problem if you are trying to target larger fish in a river with a high minnow or gudgeon population.

WORMS

Worms are an excellent bait for river fishing. Larger varieties such as lobworms and dendrobaenas are good baits for chub and perch while the smaller varieties such as redworms and brandlings will be taken by fish of all species.

SLUGS

Slugs can be a very effective bait for chub, especially when the river is coloured after a flood. They are quite unpleasant to handle, but can be held using sugar tongs when threading them on the hook.

BREAD FLAKE

Bread flake is an excellent bait for chub and large roach.

The loaf should be as fresh as possible and a piece of flake large enough to cover the hook is pinched on to the shank so that the fluffy edges of the flake extend over the bend of the hook.

LUNCHEON MEAT

Luncheon meat is a well known and popular bait for barbel and chub. It can be cut up in cubes, pressed into cylinders using a bait punch or torn from the block in irregular shapes if fish have become wary of it due to over use.

PASTE BAITS

Commercially available paste baits can be very good for most river species, particularly strong scented savoury flavours when the water is coloured after a flood.

Bread paste is an excellent roach bait and with the addition of flavours and additives such as cheese and luncheon meat it is also good for chub and barbel.

To make a basic bread paste, take two or three slices from a while loaf, remove the crusts and liquidise in a food blender.

Tip the breadcrumbs into a bowl and gradually add water, kneading the breadcrumbs until they form a smooth dough.

When fishing in cold water the paste can become quite hard and impede the hook on the strike, so I add a few drops of vegetable or sunflower oil with the water for autumn and winter fishing.

Various flavours and food dyes can be added to the breadcrumbs before kneading such as grated or powdered cheese, honey, curry powder and crushed pellets.

I have had great success with bread paste flavoured with strong cheese and dyed with red food colouring when chub fishing.

PELLETS

Small soft pellets are a good alternative to maggots, especially when trotting for roach and dace, but if the fish are not used to them, it may take longer to get them feeding.

Larger pellets can be an effective bait for chub and barbel. In particular, halibut pellets have become popular for barbel fishing in recent years.

BOILIES

Boilies, especially in strong savoury flavours, can be a good alternative to flavoured paste. While I do not think they have an edge over traditional baits such as paste, having some shelf life boilies in your tackle bag gives you the option of trying a different bait from time to time.

LICENCES AND PERMISSION TO FISH

Anyone aged 12 or over must have a fishing licence to fish for coarse fish. The penalty for being caught fishing without a licence is a fine of up to £2,500.

Full details of current prices can be obtained from the Environment Agency website, where you can also apply for a licence. Licences can also be obtained at post offices.

A licence only allows you to fish legally, it does not mean you can fish anywhere you choose. There are some locations where you can fish for free, but most fishing waters are either owned by fishing clubs that you have to join, or available to fish by purchasing a day ticket.

WHEN YOU CAN FISH

On rivers there is an annual close season for coarse fishing from 15 March to 15 June each year and you are not allowed to fish using coarse fishing methods during that period.

If you intend to fish in to the night, which can be a very productive time for many species, check with your local club or fishery to find out if this is allowed, and whether you need to obtain a special night fishing permit.

ABOUT THE AUTHOR

I was born in Oxford in 1959, but spent most of my childhood further north in the West Midlands. I am currently based in Devon in the south west of England, but still have a particular fondness for the Warwickshire and Worcestershire countryside.

I became interested in nature at a young age and spent a lot of my free time and holidays out in the fresh air walking and fishing with friends. I've lived, worked, walked and fished over many parts of Britain and that early interest has developed into a fascination for the natural world.

As well as writing, I collect and restore vintage fishing tackle. I like to fish with cane rods, centrepin reels and quill floats and when I'm not writing I like nothing more than to spend a few hours on a country stream fishing and watching birds, butterflies, and other wild creatures in their natural environment.

You can contact me and find out about my other books and current projects at my website: www.paulduffield.me.uk.

Printed in Great Britain
by Amazon